Horses
Coloring Boook for Adults

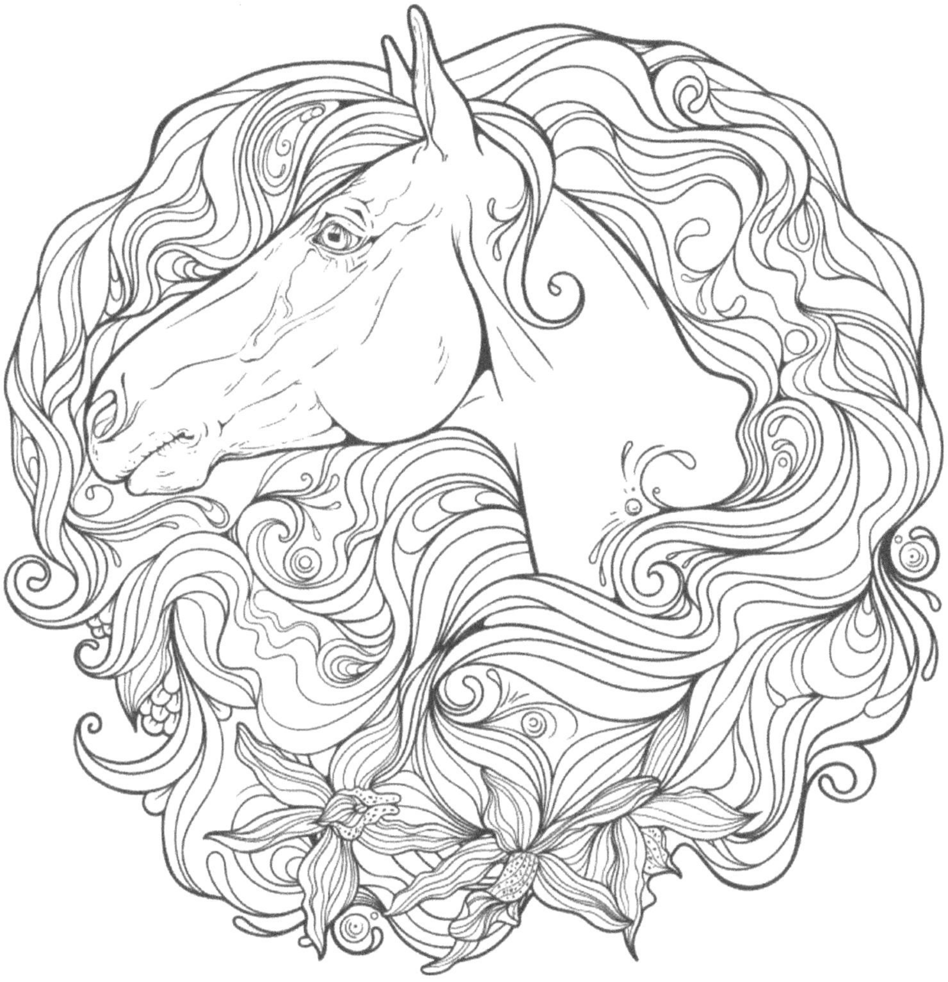

Sophia Payne

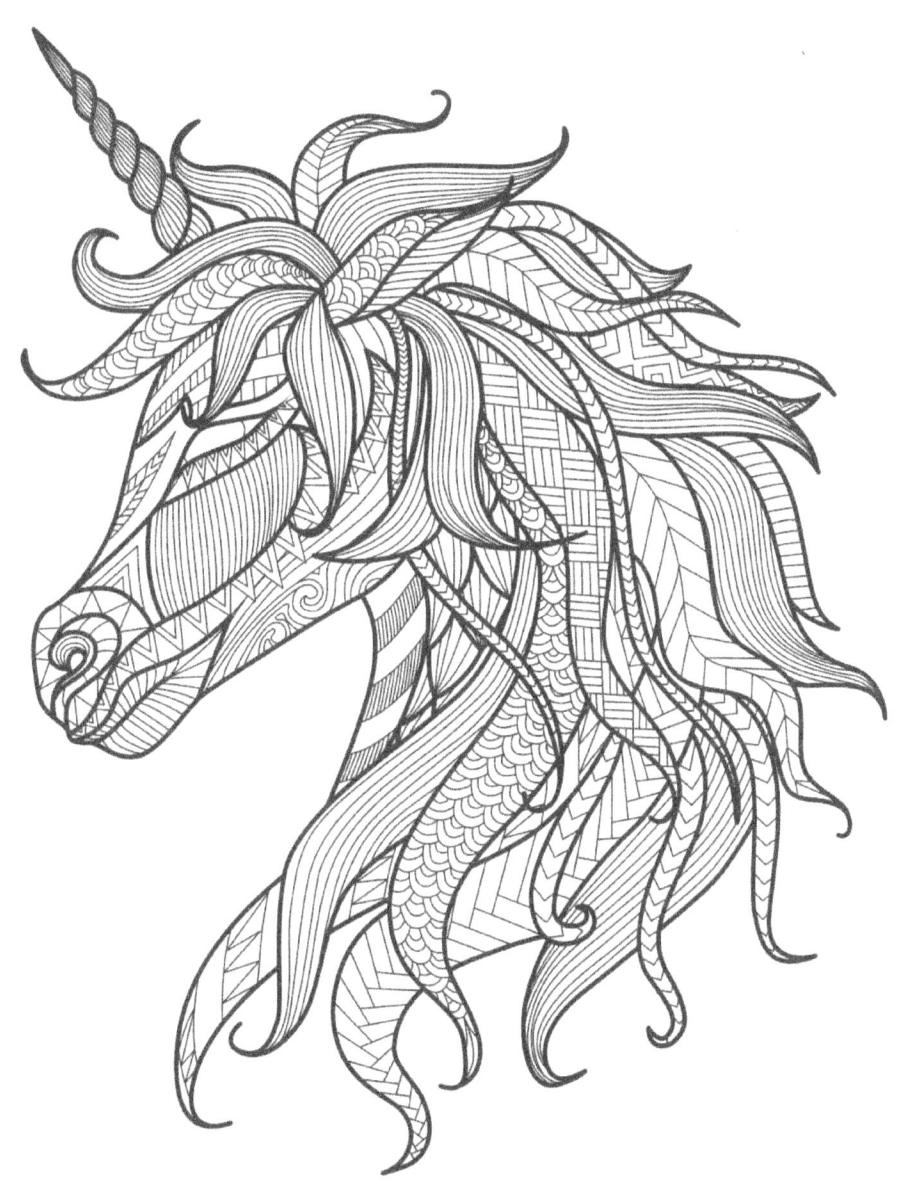

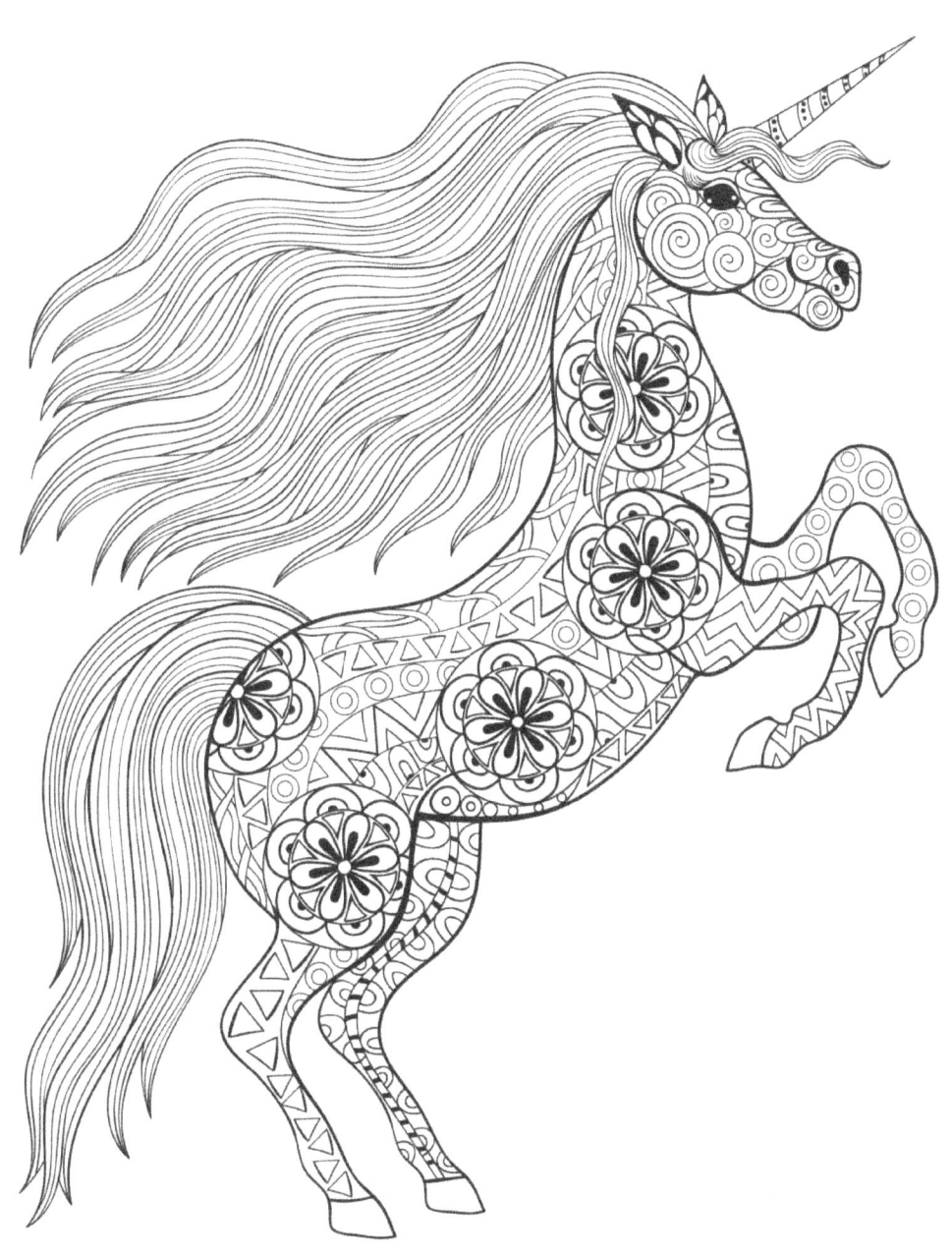

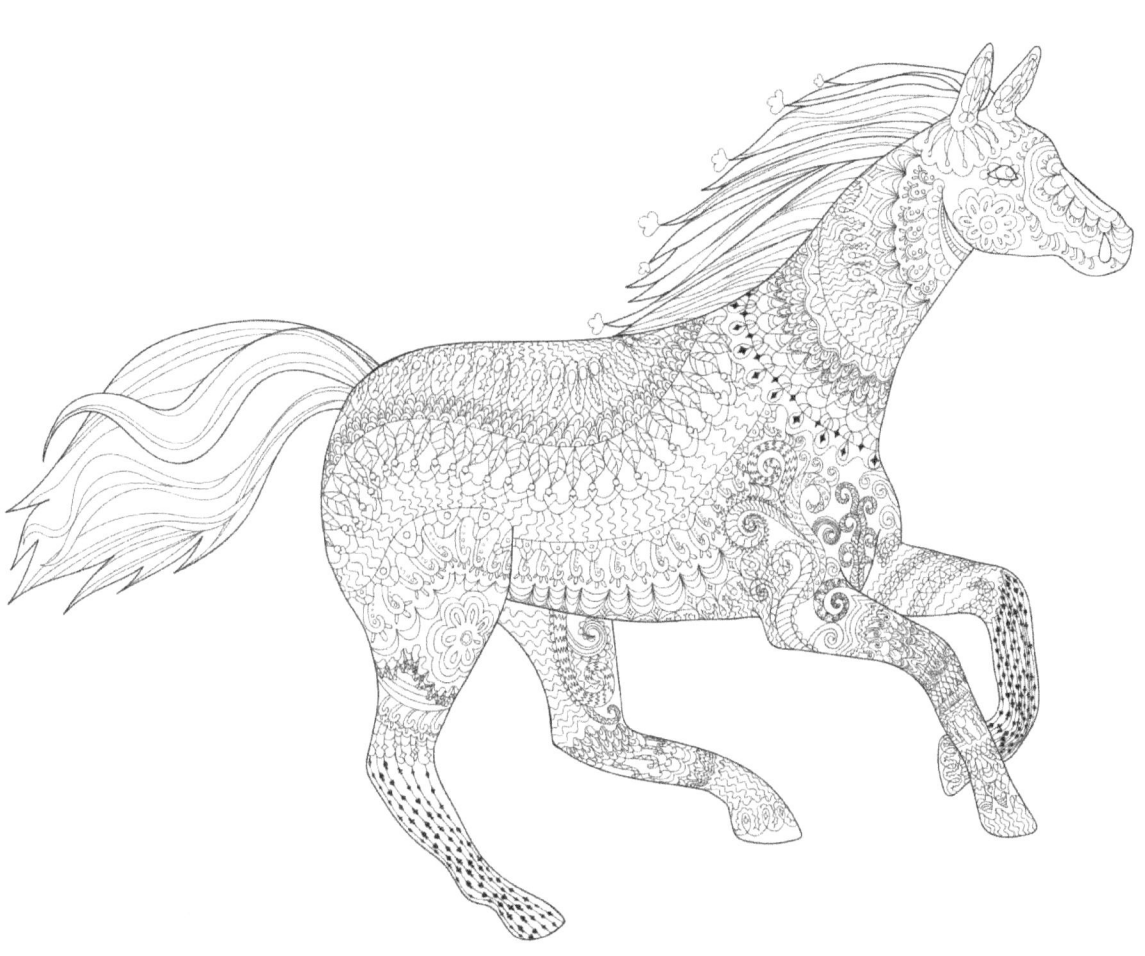

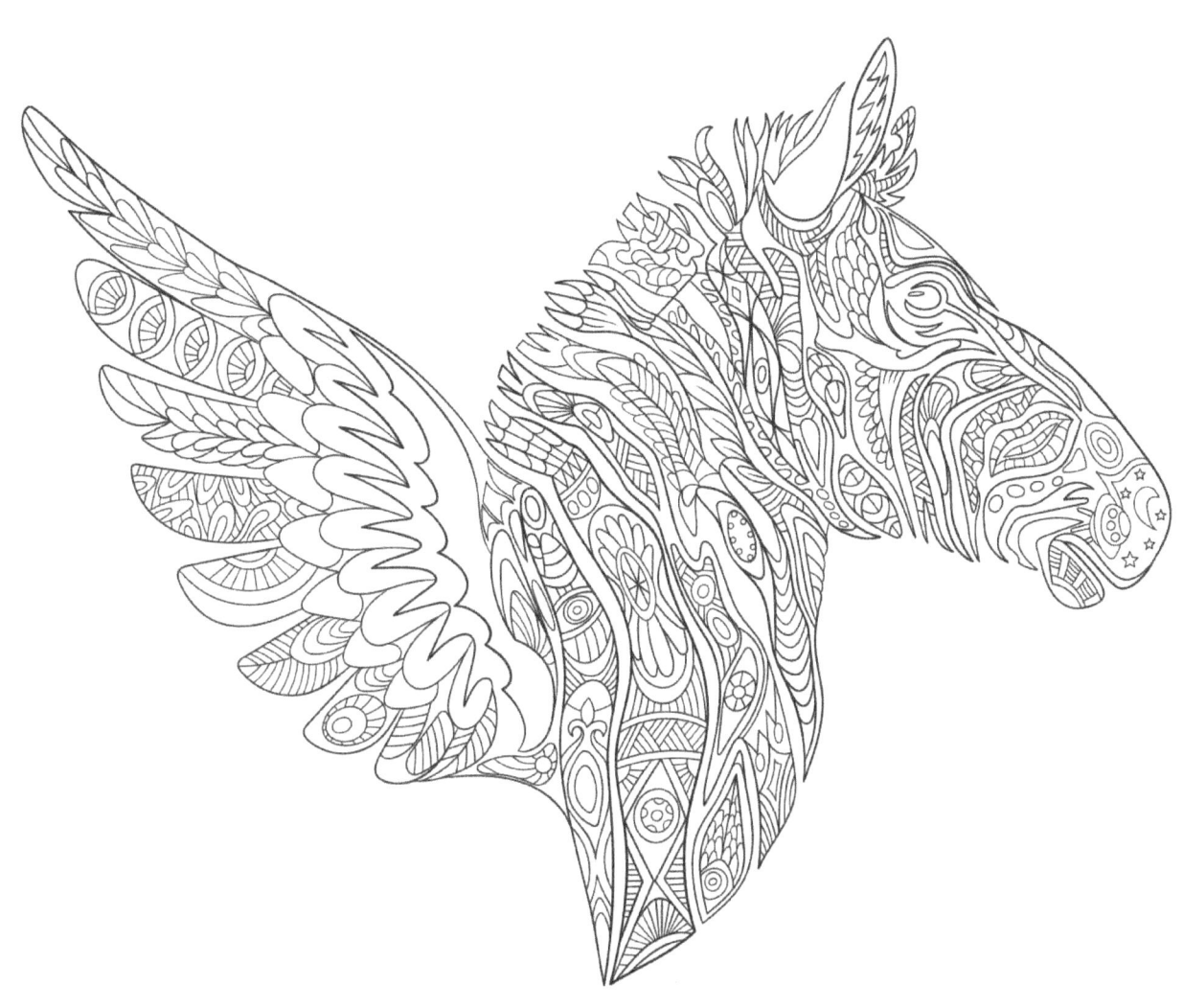

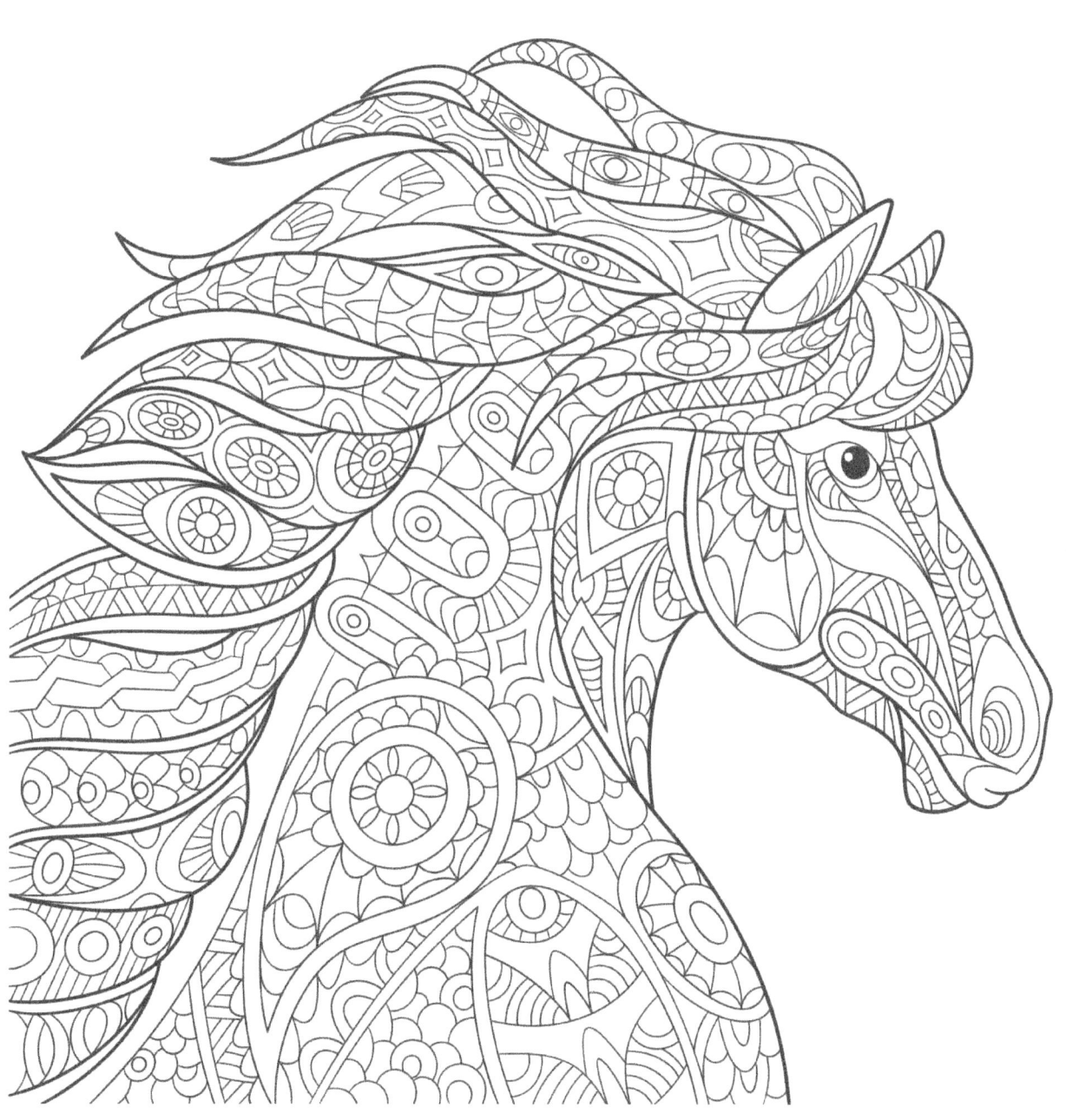

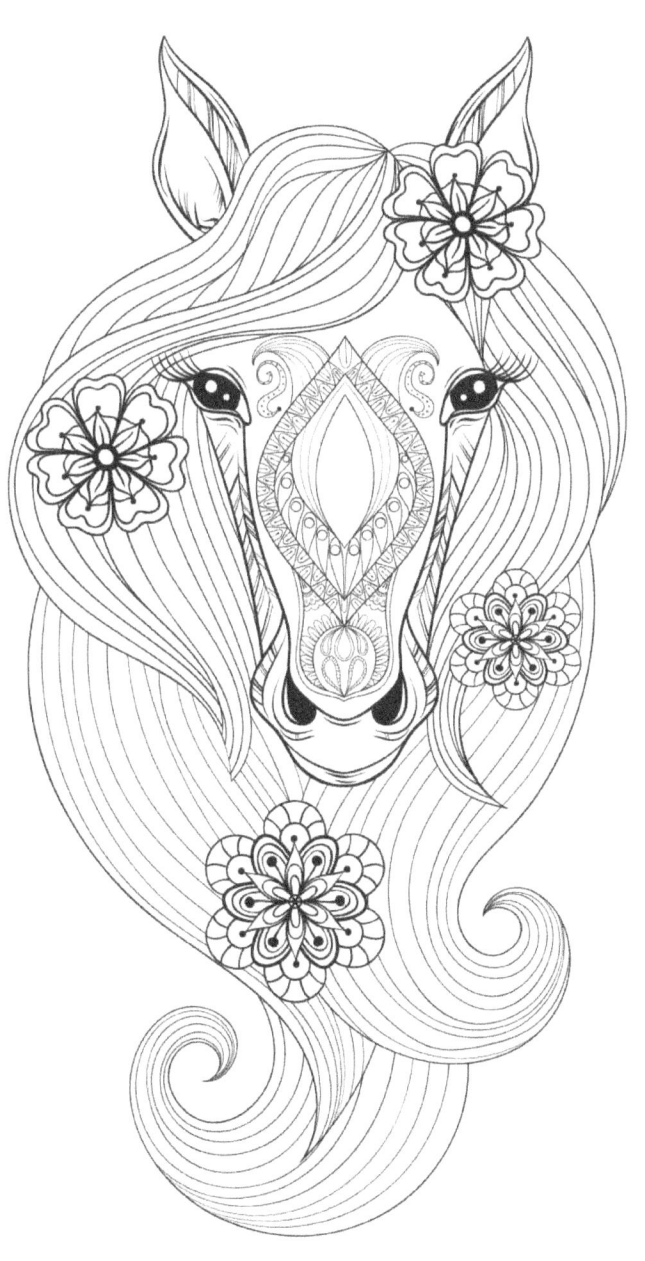

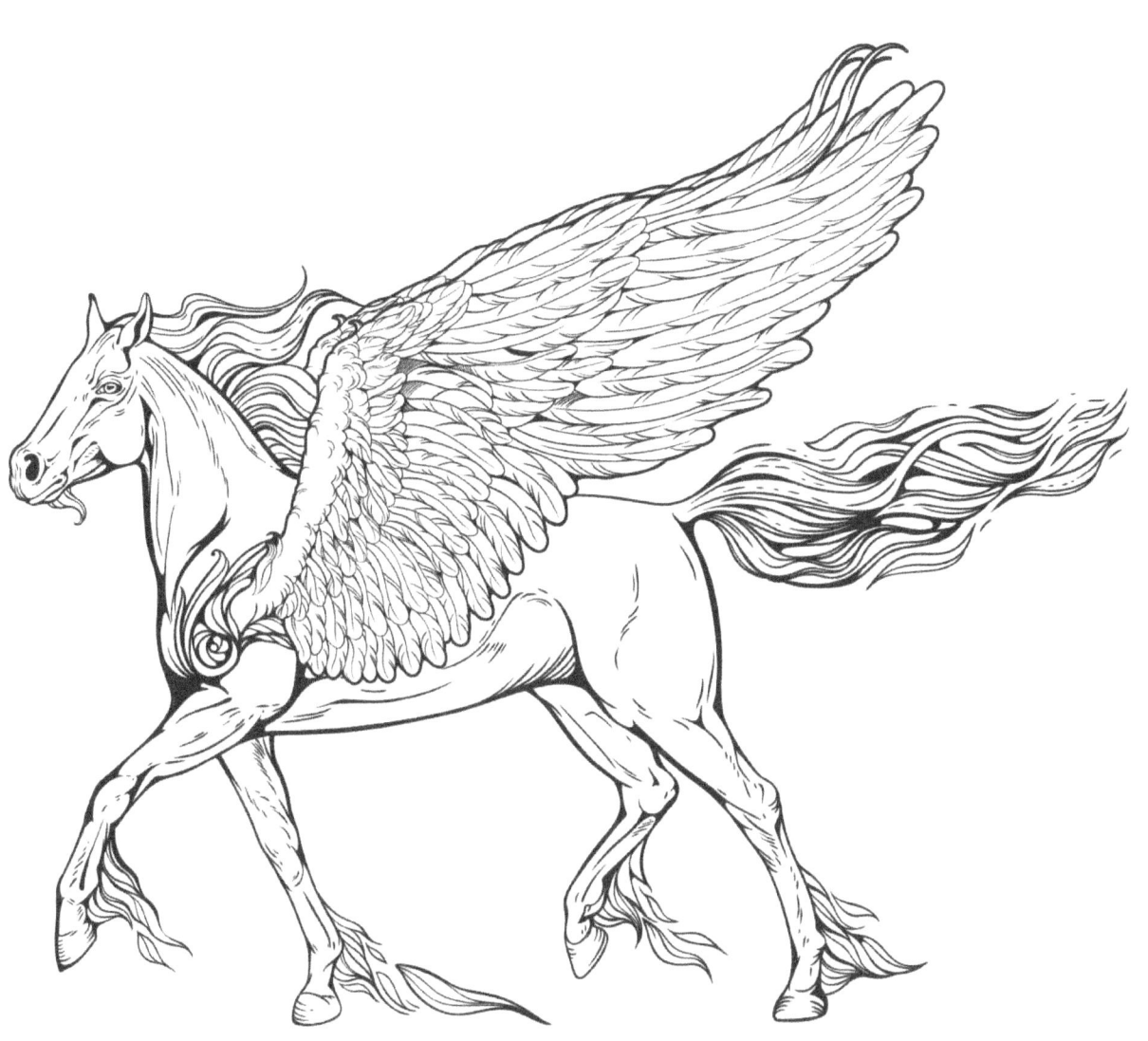

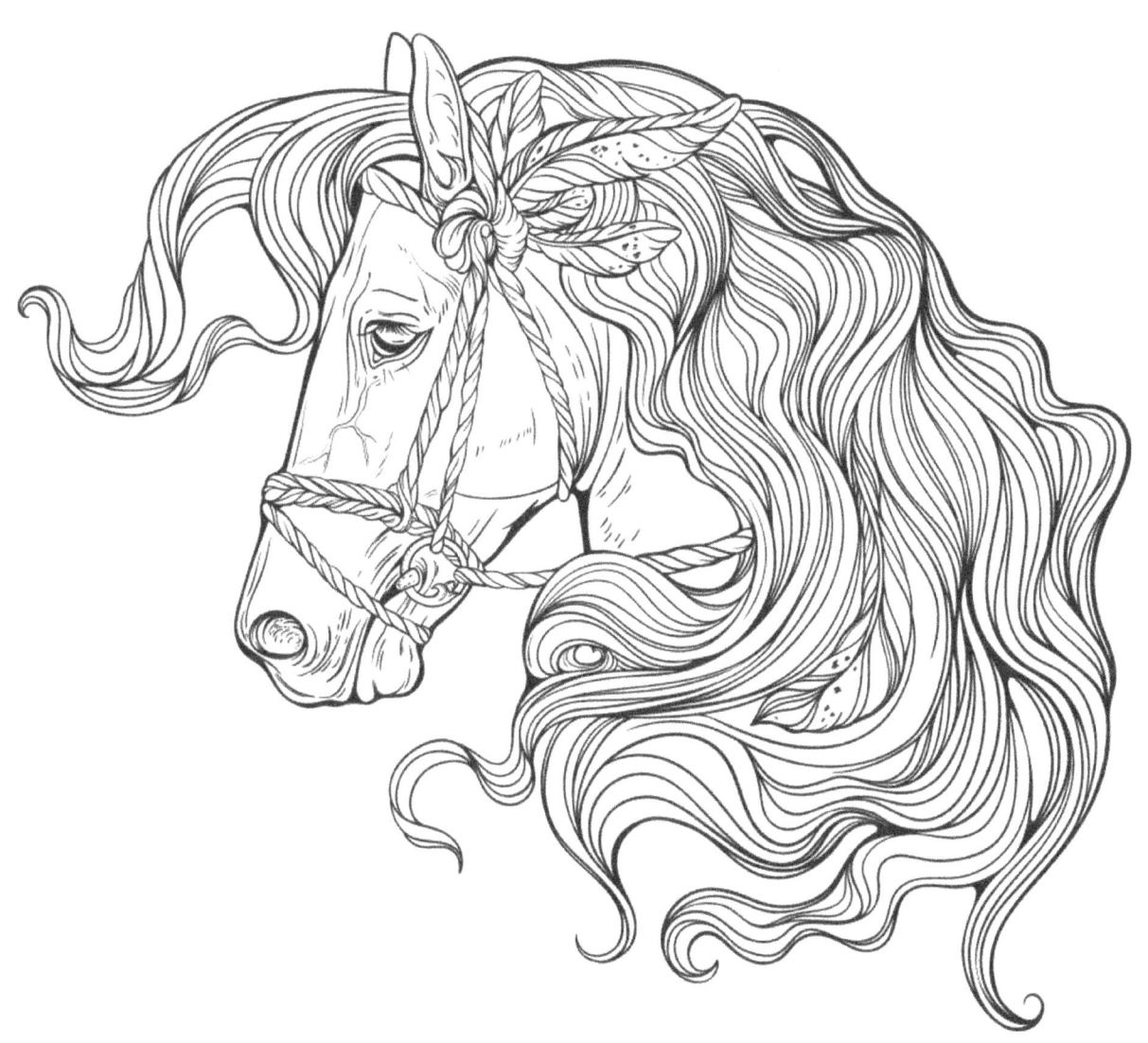

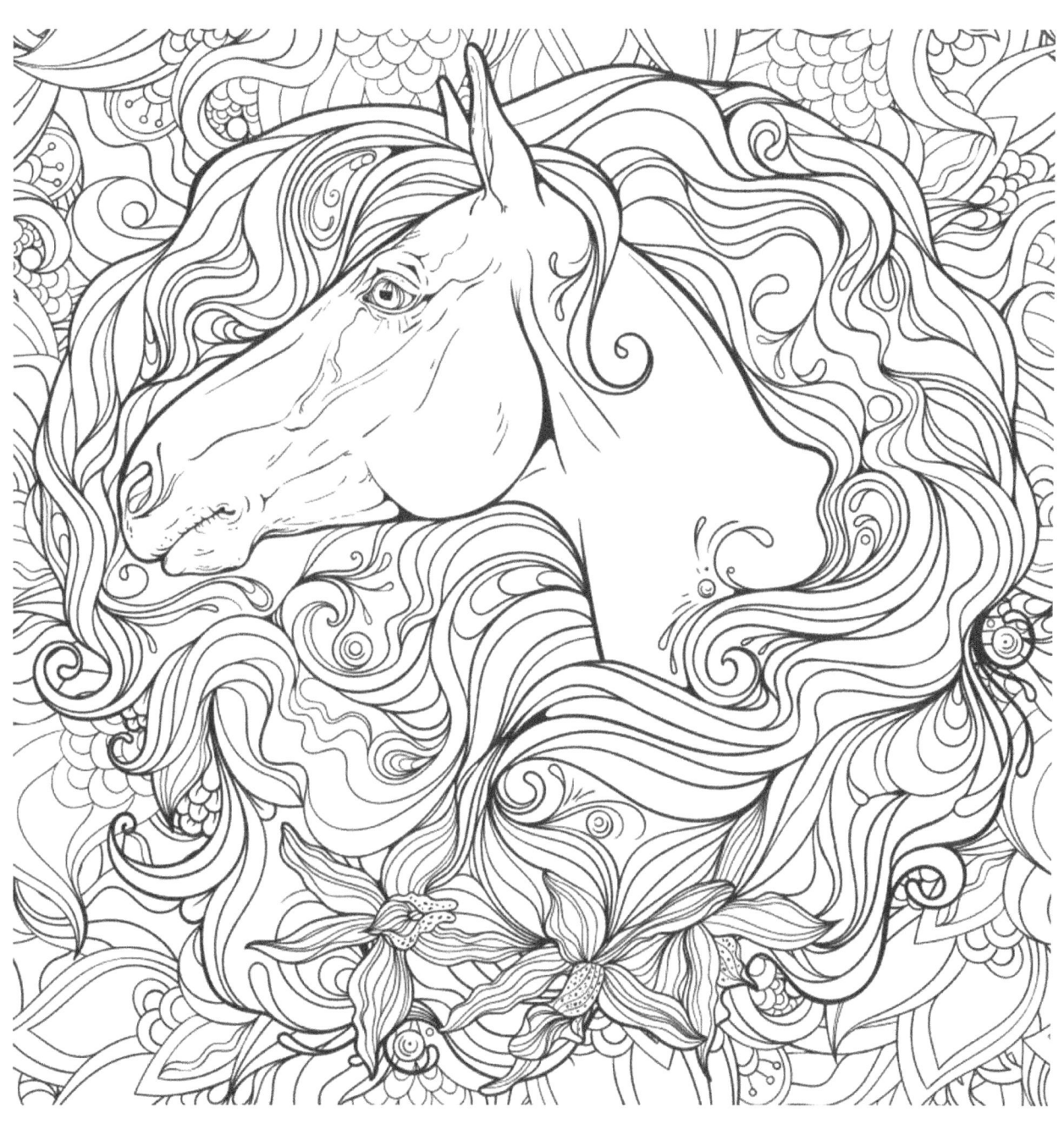

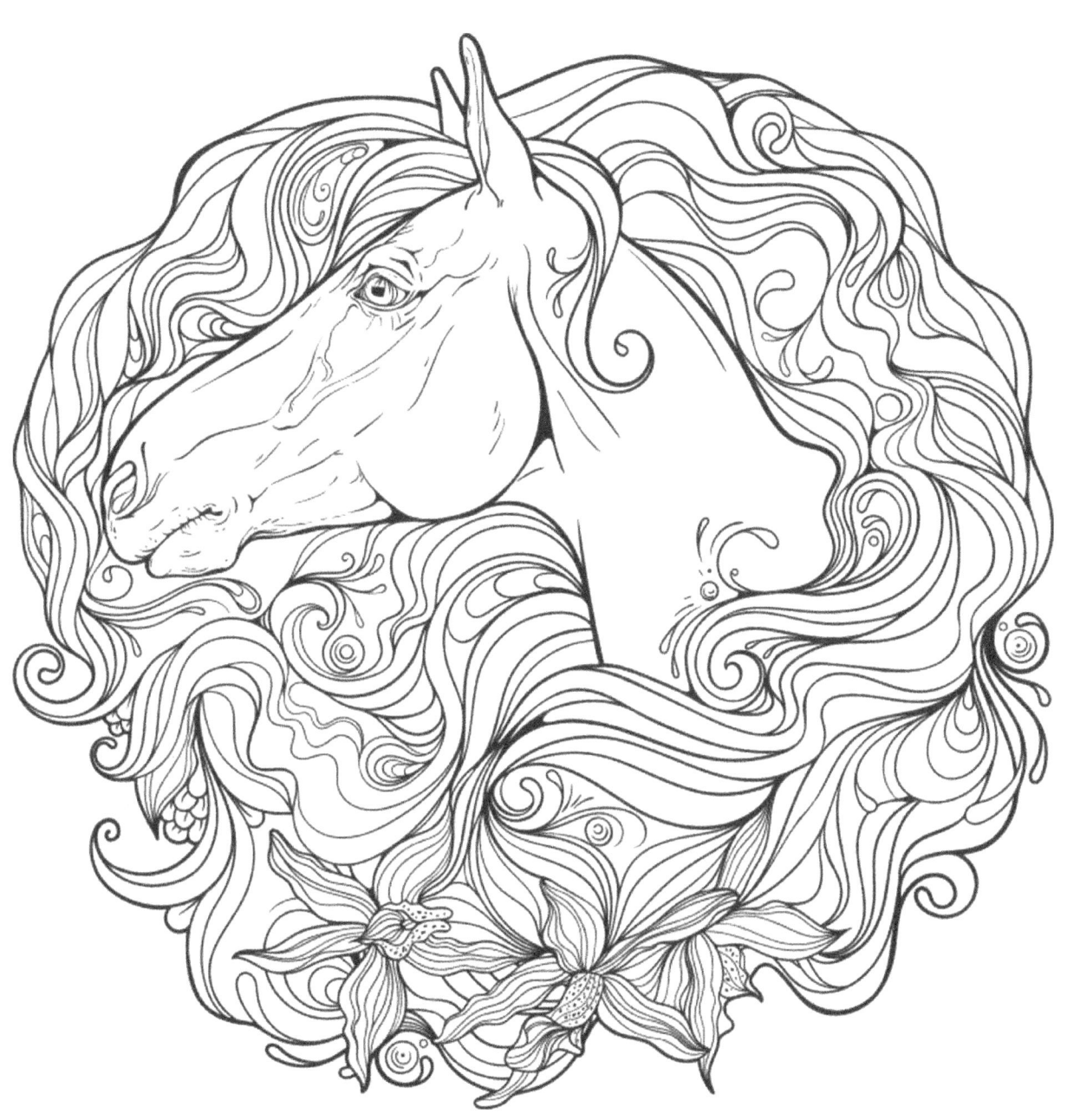

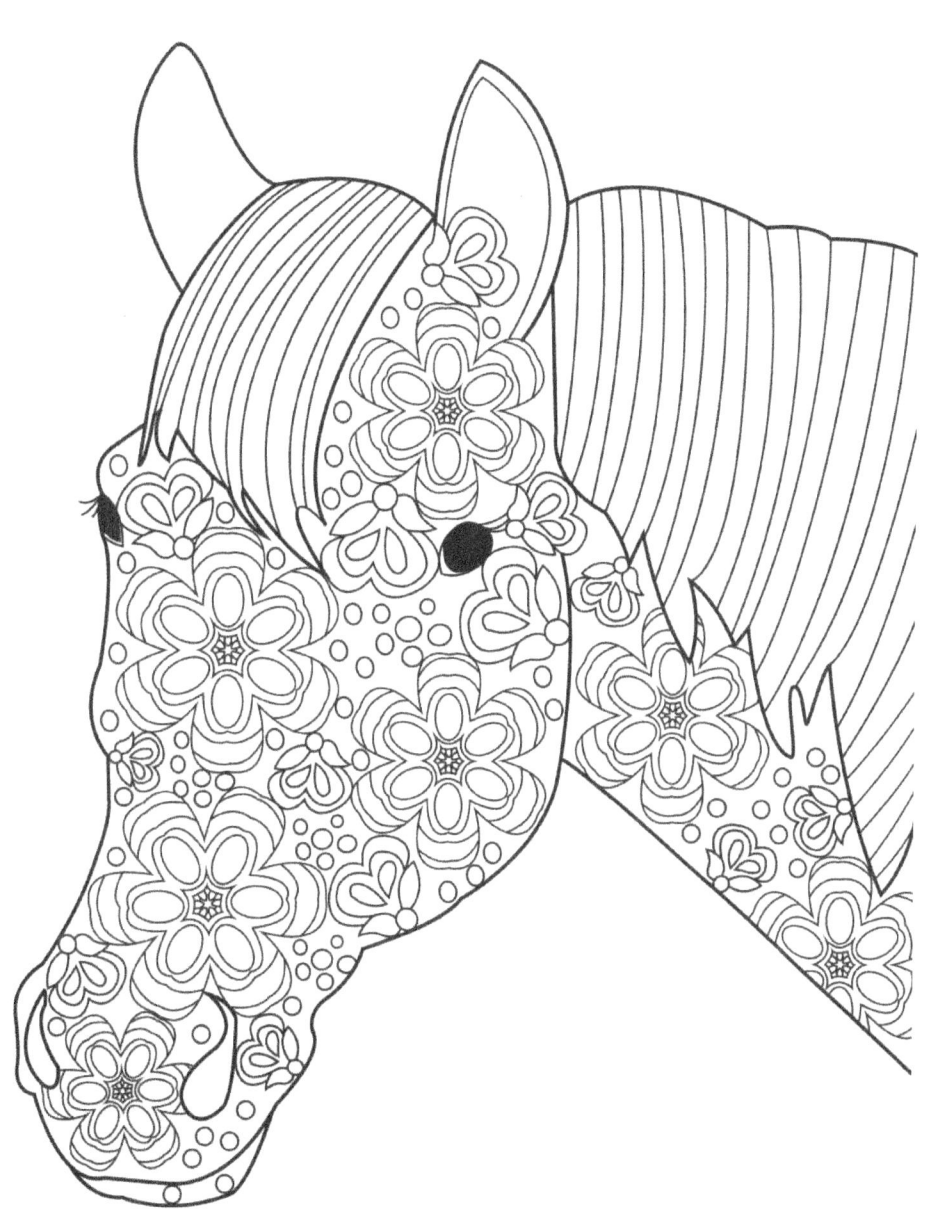

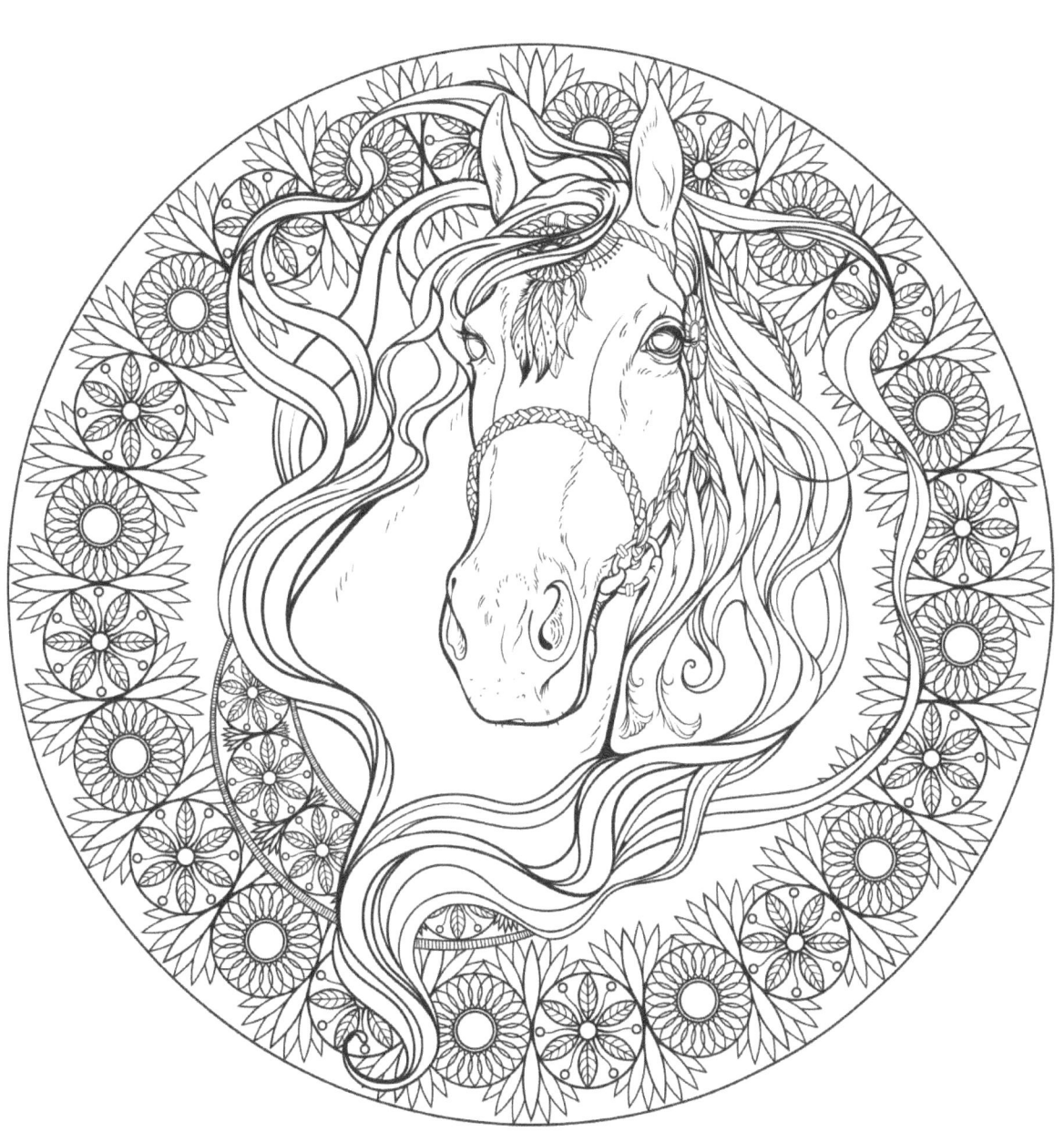

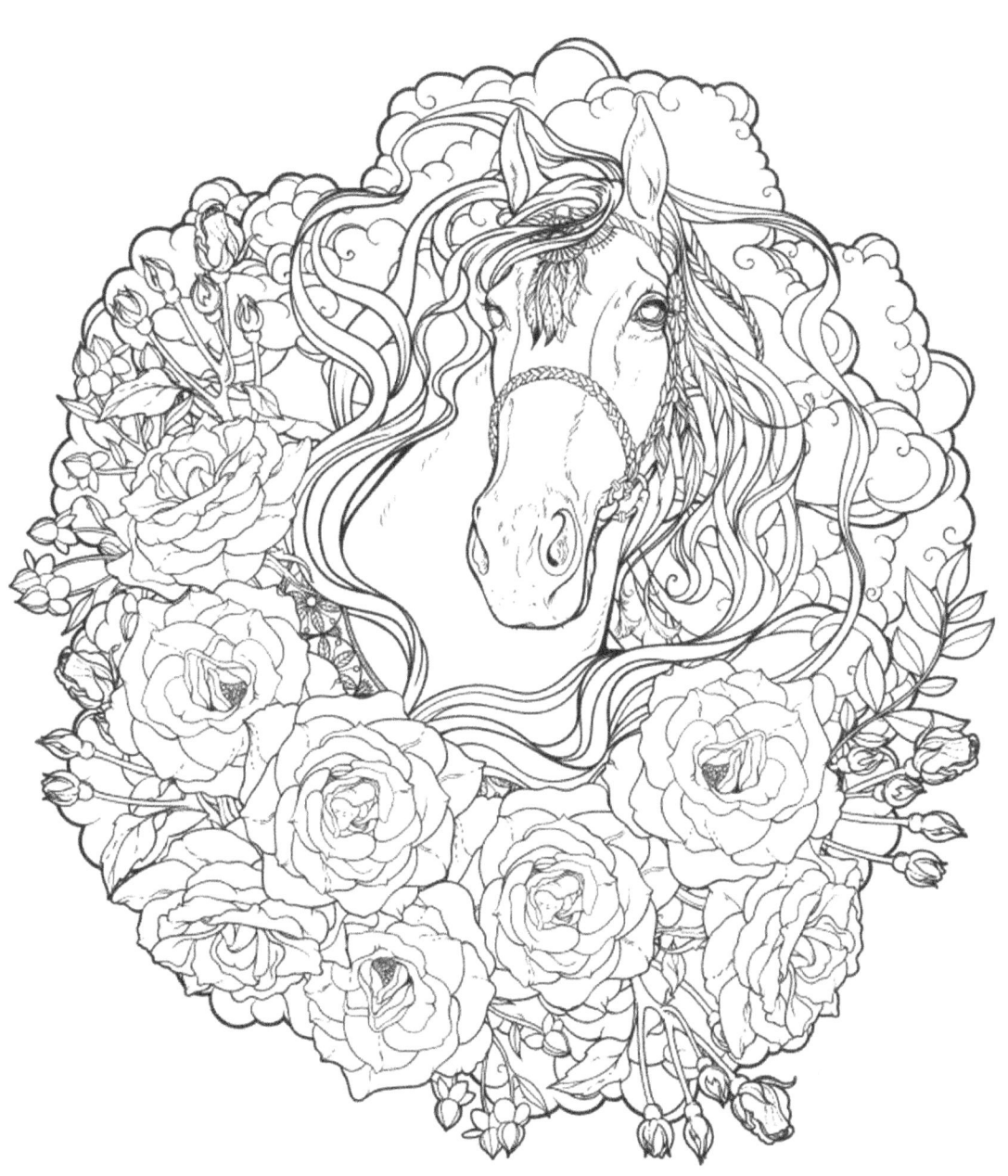

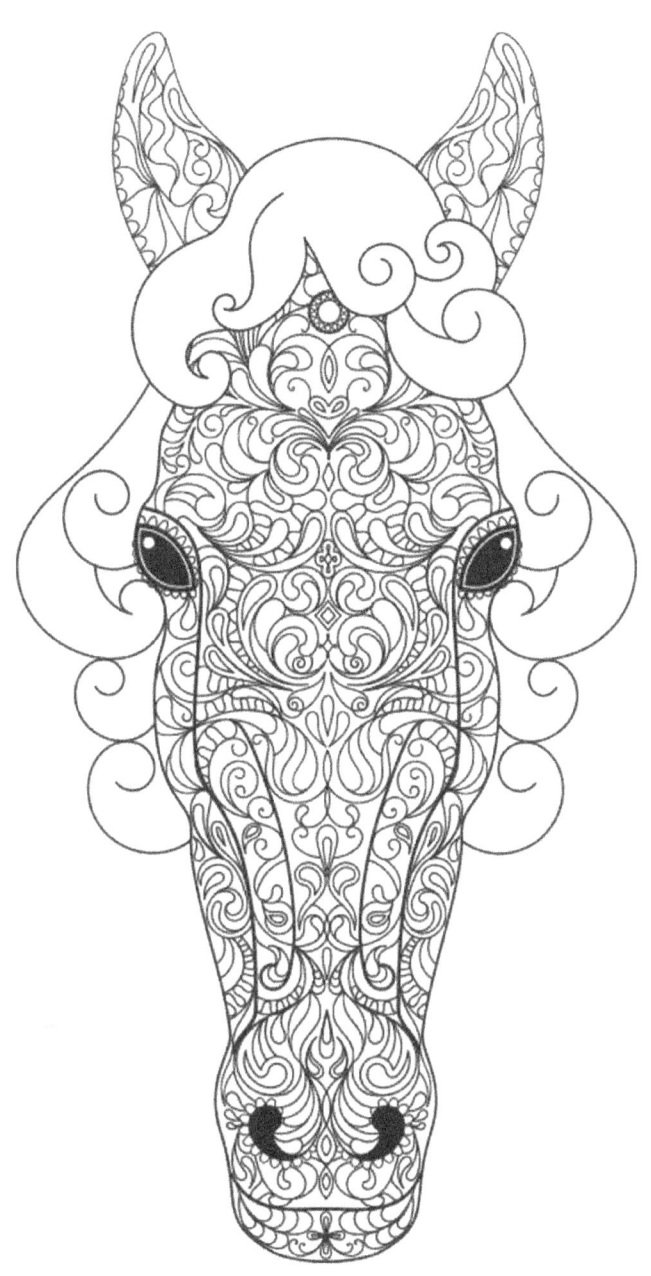

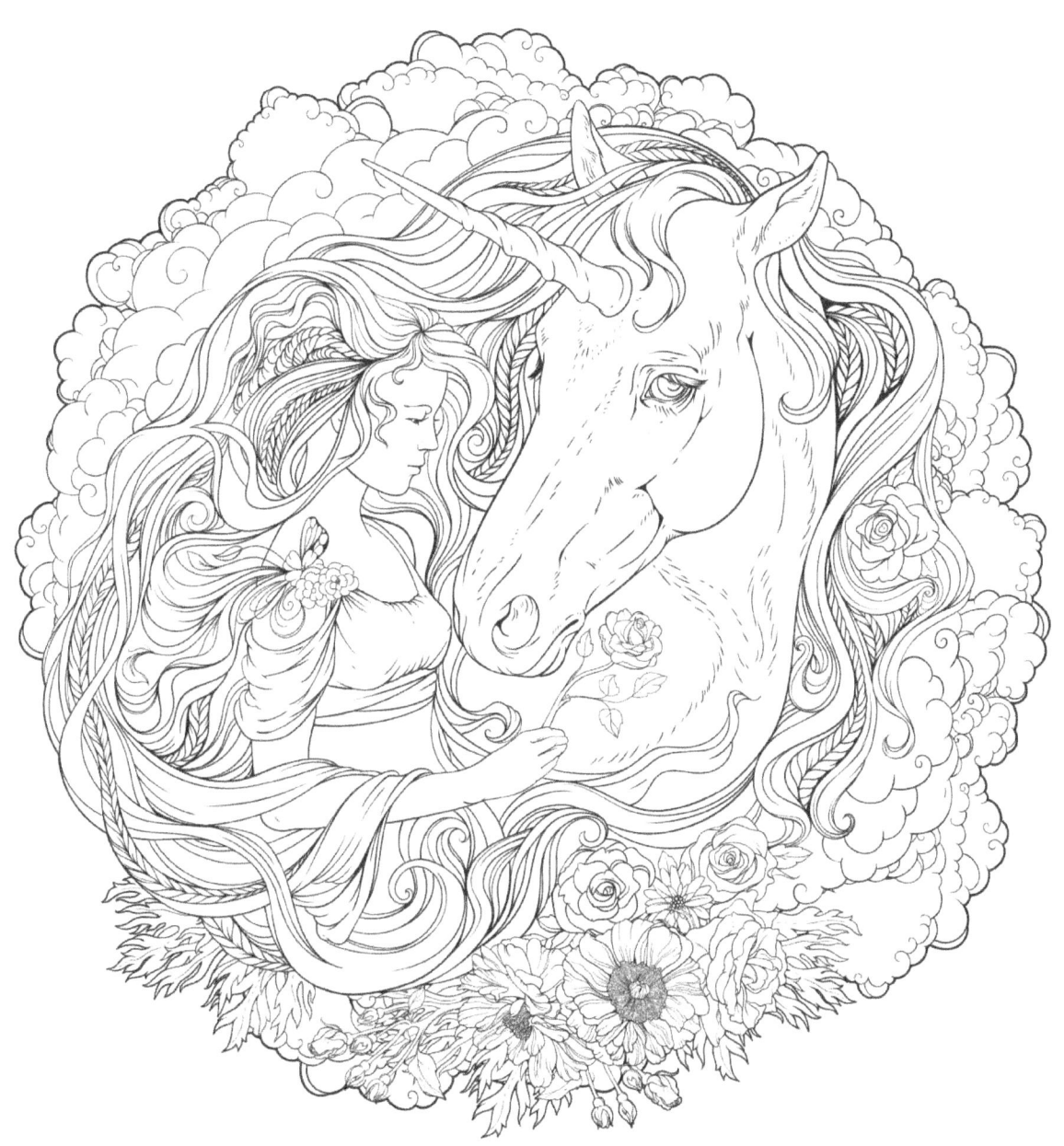

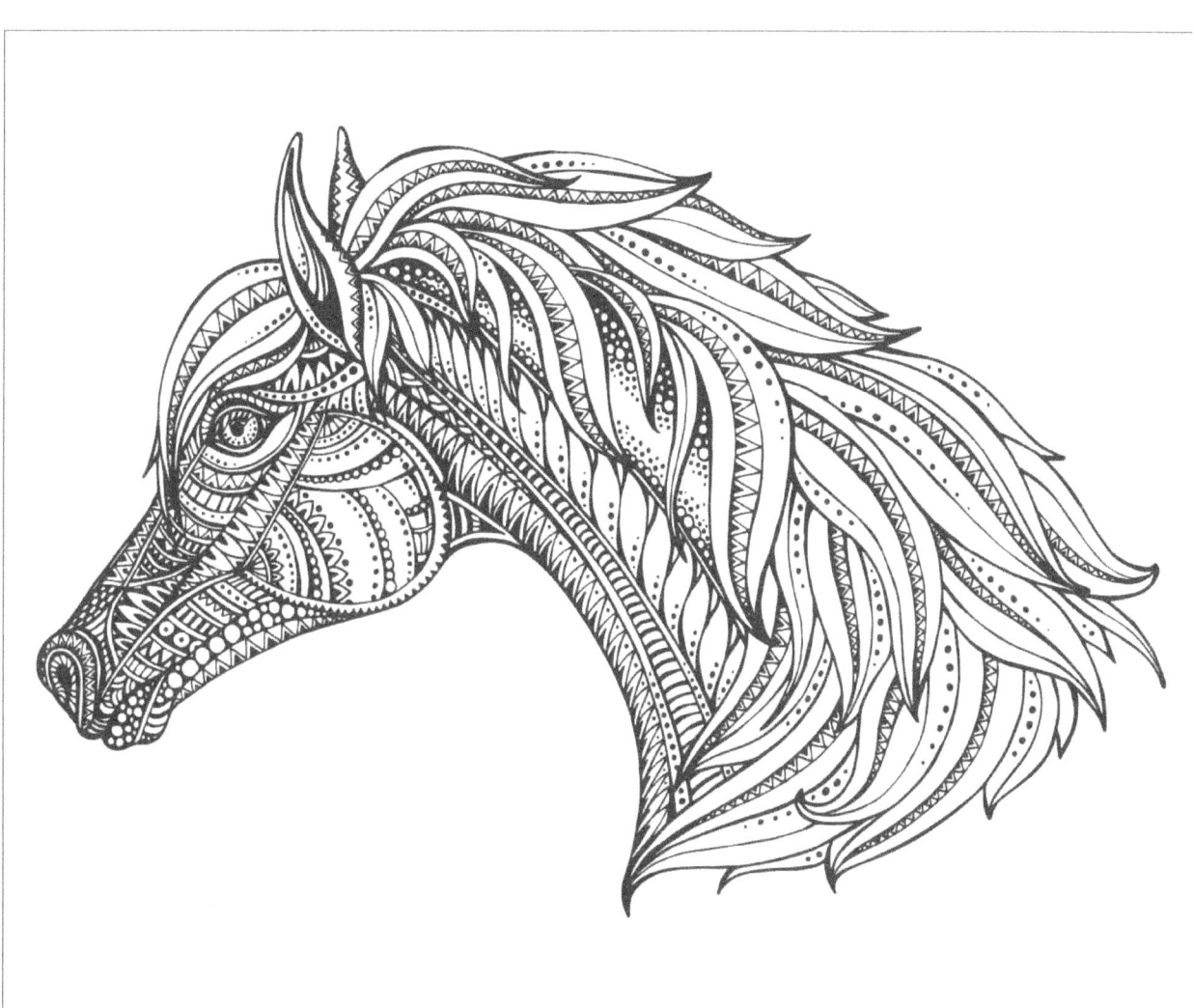

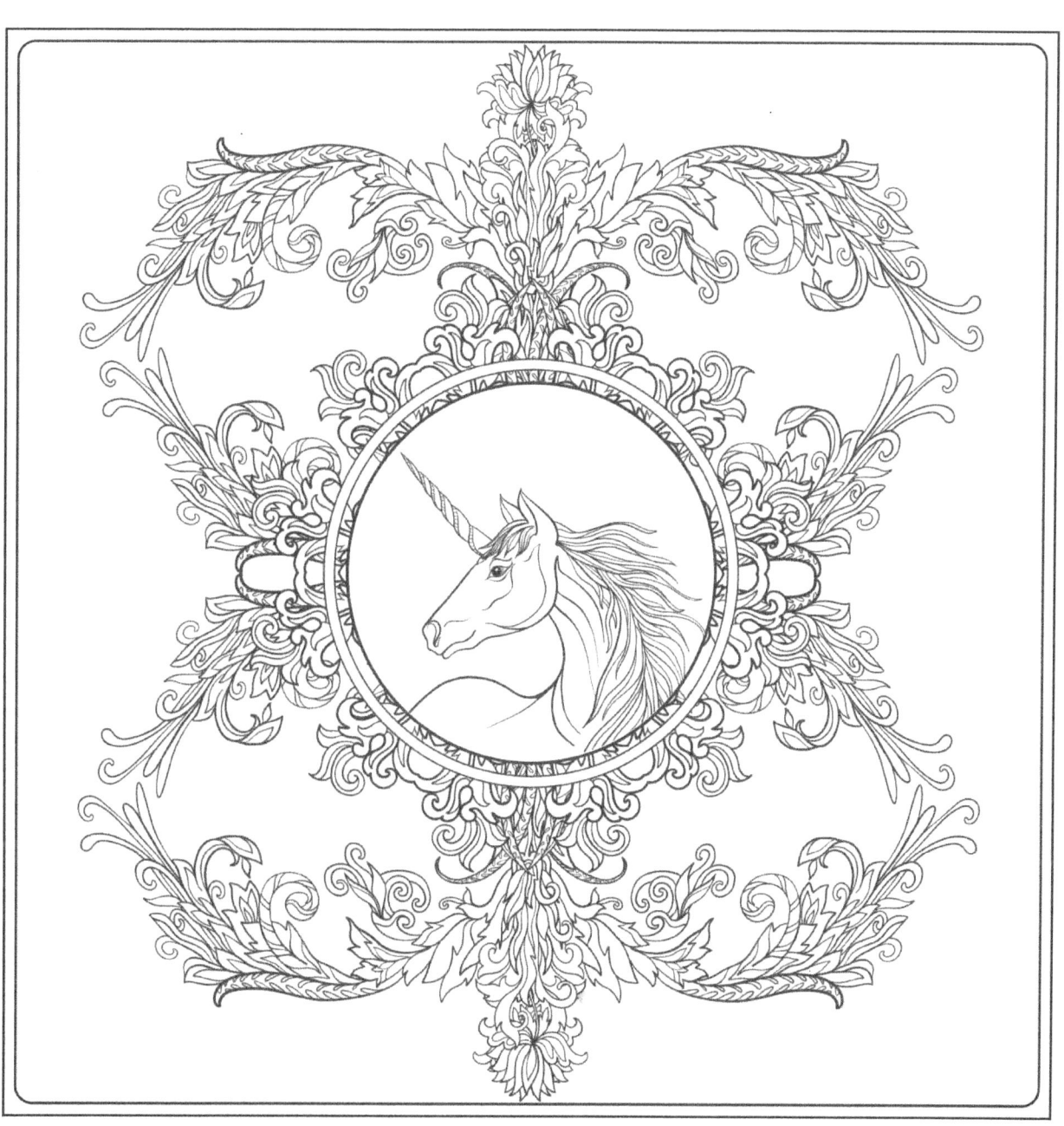

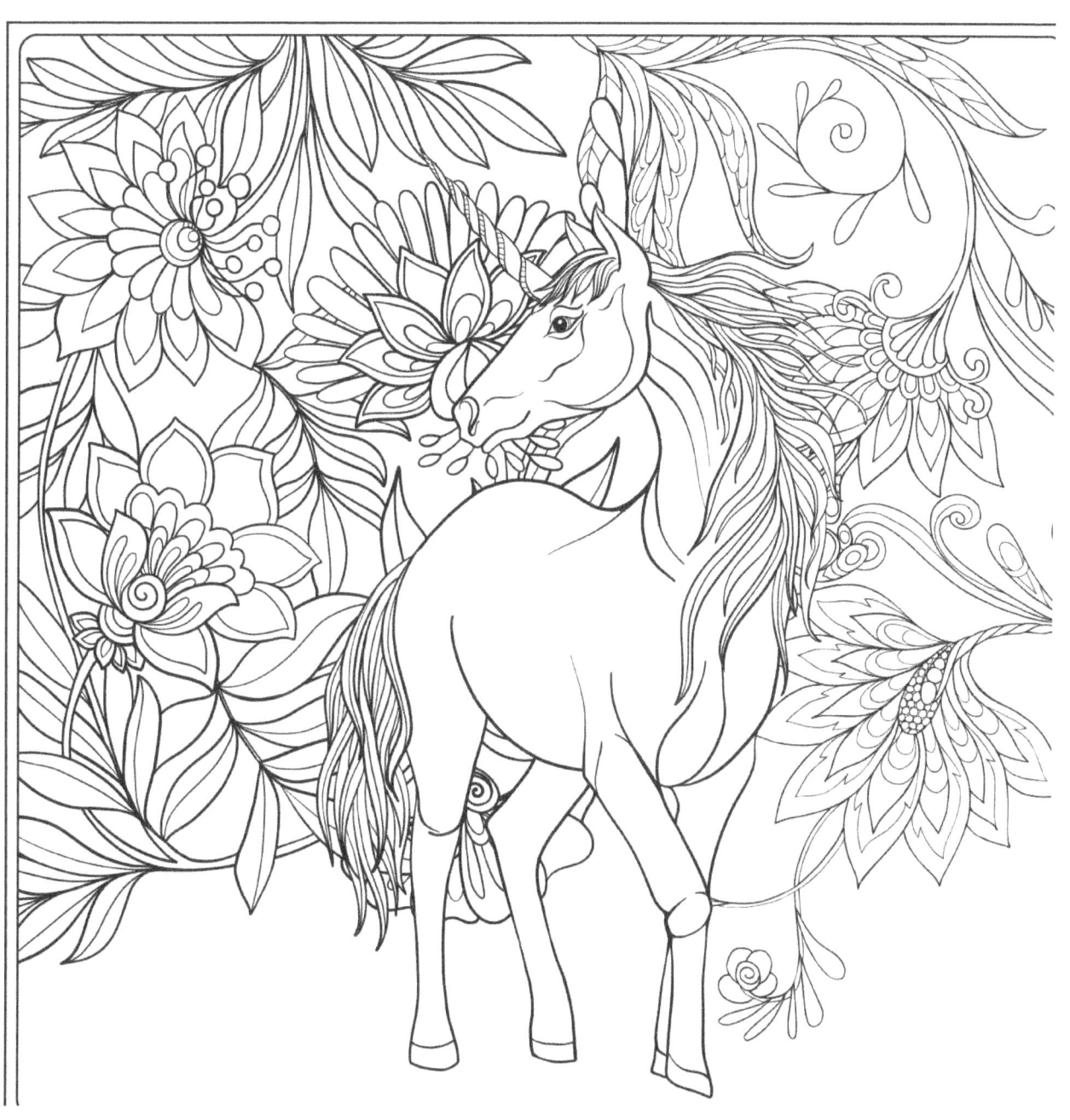

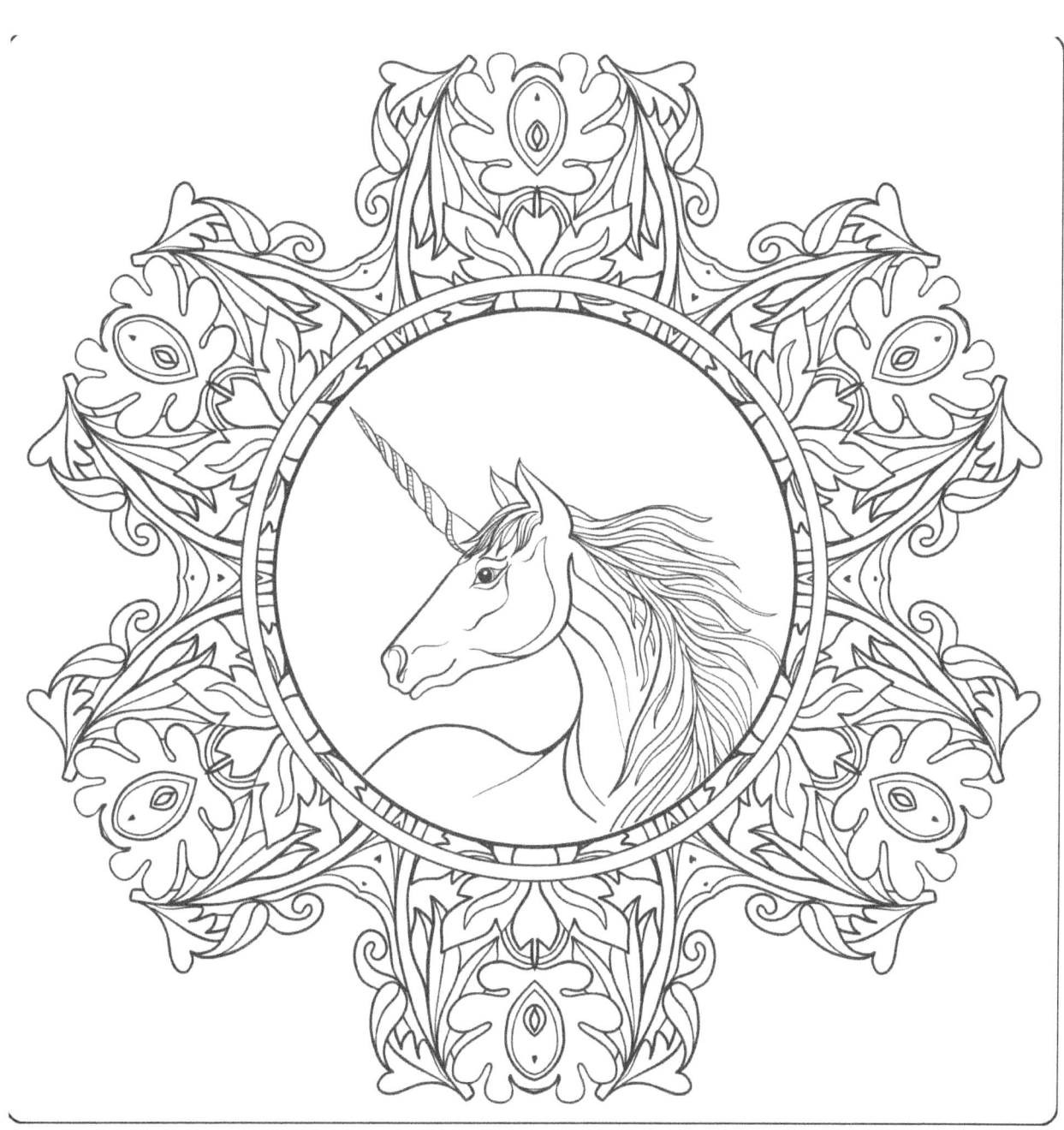

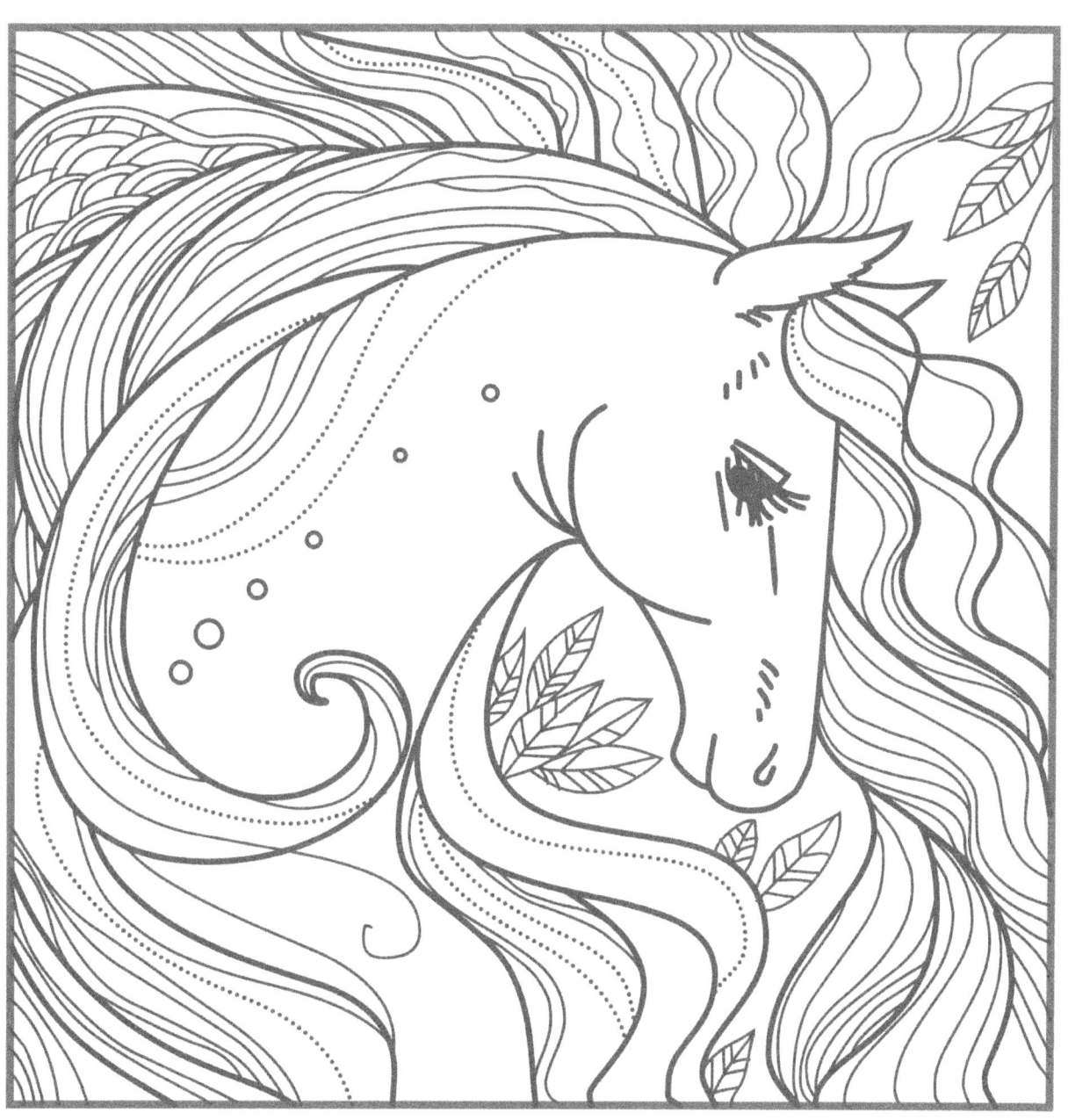

PDF Version this book : http://bit.ly/horses_c_1

Don't Miss Another our Books.

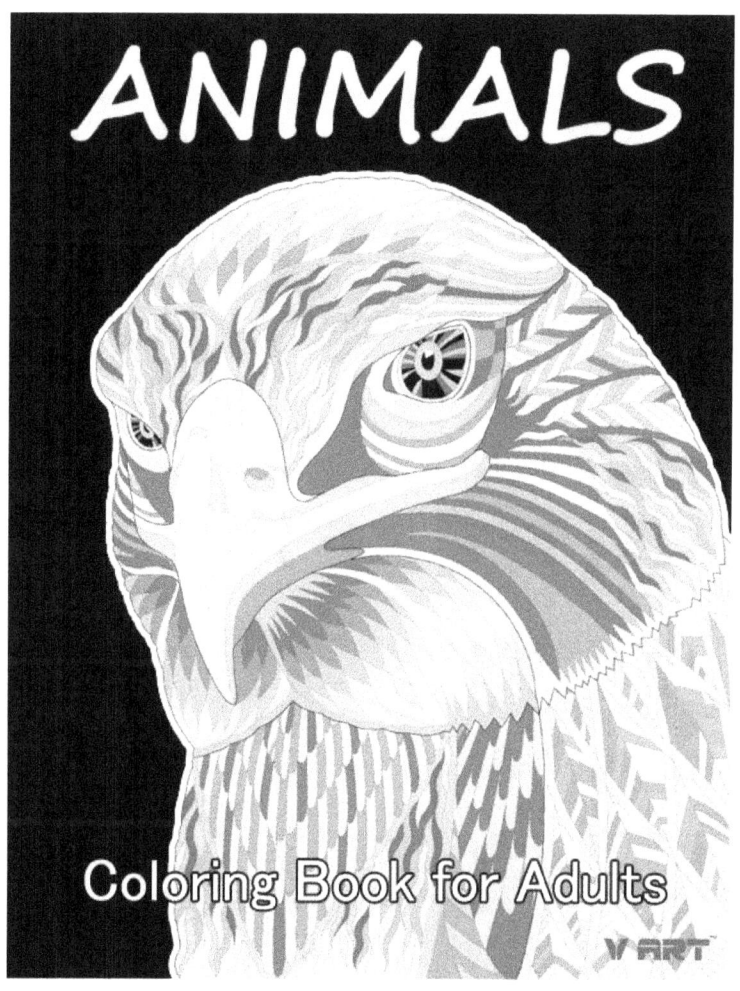

http://bit.ly/safari_coloring_b

ISBN : 9781523987931
(Use this ISBN for searching on amazon.com)